The Ballad of Lady Vigilance

Poems by Alexej Savreux

Spartan Press

Spartan Press

Kansas City, Missouri

www.spartanpresskc.com

Spartan
Press

Copyright ©Alexej Savreux, 2022

First Edition: 1 3 5 7 9 10 8 6 4 2

ISBN: 978-1-958182-24-6

LCCN: 2022949022

Author photos: Maryfrances Wagner, Wolfe Brack

Cover image: "Houndstooth" by Craig Auge

Title page image: "Lady Vigilance" by Smeza

Some of the poems contained in this book have appeared elsewhere:

"Commencement of the Elegiac" and "If I Had an Irregular Head & Were a High Renaissance Master" previously appeared in *core.* "Sunshine Beat Freestyle," "Requiem For the Train Tracks," "Catalepsy & Fantasy, Part I, II, & Redux," "A Song of Gambles" and "For Peter Tosh" all appeared in *Illogical Conceits* publications and self-published variations over the years. "Gutter Rainbows" appeared in *Shakespeare of Today* 'Les Premieres Vibes Hausse d'un Nouveau Soleil" appeared in *My Unheard September,* both of which were published by *Wingless Dreamer* over the course of the last few years.

Special thanks to Spartan Press, Jason Ryberg, Jose Faus, Sheri Hall, Brittany Noriega, Devin Edwards, Dee Jimenez, Michael T. Oakes, Lindsey Weishar, John C Sutton III, Thomas Newby, Alex Martinez, Craig Auge, and CJ Charbonneau, Craig Auge and Smeza.

Additionally, I would like to thank the fleshed angels of CSS from 2008-2019, the Prospero's folks, Teresa Lara, and Sarah Hornung, the editors at UMKC's No 1 Literary Journal, and Kristen and Duane. I would also like to thank Tom Paquette and the Paquette family, Brian L. Zirkle, Patrick Dobson, Frank Barron, John, Kyle, and Armen and the Stojanovic family.

I would like to send a verbal hug to my big sis, Bethany for being there when times were rough and mad and everything in between and for being a wonderful human

Lastly, I would like to acknowledge those shrouded in anonymity — the anonymous faces of strength, work, nurture, and resilience — I've always found beauty in the ugly, peace in chaos, and those of KCMO and KCK who are unsung and perhaps not so visible, particularly the homeless, the healthcare workers, and working-class people, please know that I remember your faces and I remember your hearts.

TABLE OF CONTENTS

Book 1: *The Apellation Poeta*
~ the MO transplant Stussy Kid & his Idiosyncratic
Gutter Poet Notebook Epic

Book 2: *As the Sun Weeps*

Oh! Time to get out the sketchbook & pencils, but NO erasers!
And there! The mechanical clock is gonna be HIM!
Da Vinci's mystery man!! A drawing of the plan;
Skeletal, superior, beauteous being . . .
On the balcony of tha drunken morning
The constitution of sobriety intact —
ascetical & protein bowls!
A roadmap into the Soul
All your metaphysical dreams . . .

~ *'From a Rooftop by Ljubljana'* in a
notebook, circa 2020

...but my own adventure turned out to be quite different

~ Frodo Baggins,
The Fellowship of the Ring

This book is for Matt, Megan, and Kevin of CSS

&

My father — for being a good man

&

Tyler

For Extraordinary Friendship

Book 1

THE APPELLATION POETA

the MO transplant Stussy Kid & his Idiosyncratic
Gutter Poet Notebook Epic

From *The Ballad of Lady Vigilance*

Commencement of the Elegiac

The downfallen, the homeless; the hungry; the jailed;
the jobless; the abused ones; the abusers who lost their
way; and those who are afflicted with illness, the ones
who are obscure but not behind an N95 mask or due
to covid but social invisibility;

       for those who are suffering reside;
The haughty; the royal; the self-important; know
that the King doesn't look at your gilded houses or
sidewalks lined with all sorts of shining symbols; The
King will be like I took a visiting Zen Bengali monk
in Kansas in as a roommate and let him live with me
for 4 months; and the people actually wept because a
stranger had acknowledged their humanity;

       When is the last time they truly acknowledged
the world's humanity? Our being sequestered shouldn't
hinder us from trying or being but soulful with hearts
of grace and gold 'twixt gilded star lilies lining our
streets like Christmas lights;

       Dear the people who look away, 2/3 of the
world crying out for help; maybe you went somewhere
and someone shoved a note into your hand that said
"Free me! Free me! Free me!" or "I'm in need" find
them a home should you choose at the very least inside
your heart you unique empathic children of flowers; be
the savior of their human needs;

       And the King will attend them through your
beautiful, radiant humanity

A Syringe in a Vein

You are neither living nor Dead
merely a jewel on mystery's crown;
your face is like a nymphy shadow;
Digging up the cold exhaust from the dying Ground
Your pearled eyes linger in realms that deify
Sight to the blind, music to the deaf,
Strength to the weak, and all Desire to Sex
Two blinking eyes flash in narcotized woe
and you exist outside a Cave of inglorious foes
On the breadth of the night's rusted wings,
Gods of parsimony unite in a cosmic matrimony
Their goddesses give birth to infantile contemporaneity
and a man dies in contentment's cradled antiquity
and life is a but a syringe full of Death
a mythical asterisk amongst the Star's ranks
its 1cc & gauge met with cantankerous skanks!
& its spoon to be the fissional division
Like an atom parceled in a box of toys
& its half-hearted security an honest conviction
of your poppied needle screaming in your fat vein
nothing but a screeching willow
an opiate who seldom dreams of cannabis
and a dazed head on Destiny's Pillow,
milky dew found, head hit the ground
Let the lights dance, headrush in a trance
Nothing's changed, but your gaze is eviscerated
A Galactic birth of a Godly changeling

Wrought Seas of black soot, bringing time
to my stately home in the scented Sun
where the end eventually brings everyone
and I am sure of nothing but methadone's desire
Beyond oblivions whimpering apocalypse
Like a caryatid unworthy of her pillar
Lies in an immutable pale Horse that can't be tamed
and an ecstasy stolen by villains
Just like a fat needle screaming in a fat vein!

If I Had an Irregular Head & Were a High Renaissance Master

I have an irregular head, muse & vassal & as I slept on
    naked silk, with my mistress by my side,
 I transposed I separated from my body & combusted
    out of existence,
temporarily, in my new self of non-existence,
I decided to paint all night & into the day, so I went forth,
& I left rhyming schemes to the Poor, I picked up my
    paintbrush
and I invested (decided to paint) brownish icicles on my
    commanding canvas
& I gave (painted) the angelic Girls Orange-plaid Wings,
& little Girlish smiles, & their frizzy Hair Augmented
    their affections Still!
& their Special Grins, livened the raw hands of my self-
    created jowl! ~
But as I sifted unhearted grins on their innocent, glowing
    Smiles,
I thought of the painless edict of God's own Eden,
The Freedom Nest's own hyped-up fortress mote on the
grand dawn hearth & the didactic grey clouds beyond all
the Suns that Float!

Catalepsy & Fantasy Part I, II, & Redux

1.

I think as though I am in a strait jacket
an immodest luxury to cometh, an emotionless sigh
cigarettes on the dazed, occult sofa
Glass pipes, the momentum of history is heathen,
Because she doesn't die
Sublime, she may be, perfect figurine, (at last I have seen!)
& Brazenly, I remove my logical monocle

2.

A glass eye she screams & ends the darkest of nights
Maggots await, unbroken knot, time is stuck
& vanity is quite illuming & ill
Zounds adhere! Be still! Charity's prosperity!
A mouthful of sex strapped in luck
Right before a blighted dawn, my vigil alerts a street
light & iron rain
I cometh to right before the incurious wrong

3.

Neither heaven nor hell shall ably tell
My mystery ends in a swell, a riot of periled calculus
Its own psyche is ignorant, self-effacing
Like a biography transient, a vision's utterance
Suns! A loud fluttering, drone by the seaside
A disaster upon the disheveled ears of yore!
Spells that shall impart wisdom upon folklore

4.

& the knees that clash, oft past suicide's grasp
    Joker hats on those jackals!
A great length of rope shall hang them from their
    doom's mast!
The elements of idleness slowly arose & those idiots
have swindled my love, & eaten her bones
I am still, unheard & unrecognized by tongue
Sleight of hand shall entrance, anti-implants

5.

Past all opiated Afghani perfumes & Tibetan oils
I have become a self-seeking, sustainable pariah!
To vanish from the land, like a handful of sand
A mast with no evident sail; winds, noise stuttering
    soft & low
& Chemistry is so obviously prevalent, a calamity of
    design
How it embraces, dislocates, & retraces a damozel

6.

She is history's magnifico song, canto, an opera!
A chain smoking almah & style cunning, a fiend!
I am a conjurer of the stoned & communal audience
A fantastic spectacle, in an unending hour glass
I awoke to the tribunal, a haze, I light a candle
& Right before my eyes she sullenly awakes
Upon her shivering breast plate, I eat the first bleat

7.

Much she affords me, though I could never offend her
But brought on by time's nuisance, a relative construct
I'd laugh until my rioting rubbed itself out
But she doesn't dream in miscellaneous ways
She is the vain, incalculable, modern desirous
She is a modern lover, born of incredible, nubile hands
Don't forget her past loves became the damned

8.

But could such a tortured eye bear to sulk?
In infamous interrogations, knotted like discarded silk
& Once in a great while, my droning eye could transcribe
Down in history, with a vile pen & a vial of iniquitic juice
Just so much to destroy a submissive self, like art
I never had the balls to cum oil masterpieces
Galvanizing, she left in a brothel of despair

9.

'tis whereupon she discovered some crystalline dares
Unfair, she climbs up the side, like a virus that rides
on top of ye, unafraid of hell soaked, improper, pisces
She, above all else is made of those which a-soak
Don't forget the harmonica breath as it wept & I awoke
So calm thy veils for once in awhile
She breathes & bleeds with song, til I crack a smile

10.

Crafting an affair, in arrears like a commodity with a fetish
She is also solo gone, the days of rear worn comedy down
She is illogical, I am saintly, infirm & charm'd
But whence does this propensity eek to flow?
Unconscious she does it again, & I beg for a moan
Quite witless I am, but then again what is it to you, friend?
I hold a revolver to my head, I am electrified, inculcated

11.

& with this 36 caliber machine & unself creator
I spin the galactic chamber, inside a bullet like a universe
Makes for the best of loving, on trial, like a felon
I click out for the time being, nobody though will ever
    get out
She checks the bullets, I pull on the strong winds
I nail myself to the wall like a hypodermic parasite
I'm told to run, but I haven't got the legs

12.

I'm no longer worthy of her downtrodden gait
If pleasure be the meeker, & the seer the cleaner
Then perhaps we should strive to behold a believer
Right in the cockles of our palms
Til she bleeds & bleeds & there's grass growing on the lawn
This be your domain, your infantile crown & just
You have swayed young fiend, to the infinity of dust!

13.

I have cut off both of my hands so I cannot masturbate
It's how I will come alive in the future
My belief in self-torture is only a fractured, dissident eye
Witnessing the trickery, horrors, & vestals of time
A eunuch should be allowed to attain that mystical gain
Whereupon love is aptly misplaced
& then! Ah, yes, for that definitive emotion! I shall no
    longer guess thy cursed name!

14.

I am a nobler man than I was in those days
Just the same, I was torn apart leaving maggots in my brain
they gnawed & gnawed, my brain outgrew their game
like a Chessmaster destroying a checker playing gnome,
as neurotic as a court jester smoking the rock of crack
and yet there I amazed, awaiting an injection of
    something to bring me back
. . . and I lay in that trance, in that dream, in that
amazement,
for a momentary eternity . . . never having once realized
    the difference.

a.k.a. Bathtub for Unclean Infantes

The only dirty water I will submit to be drowned or
    bathed in is the mythic sea of incontrovertible
    fortune
For it is the only dirty water that cleanses beyond
    comprehension and leaves no trace of filth, ah, but
all bathtubs are left with filth.

BAPTIZE ME, O, Shepards!! And Franciscan Monks!
    Wont for long?

    . . . I don't want to be buried.
I want birds to eat me corpse while I lie rotting in a field.
Aha! And so there!

Perfect & Grotesque

But what else could be realistically said?
The funeral of life is the death of the soul and the
    failure to fly

...& the preference is a breathing tapestry with more
    harmony & grace than the totality of the High
Renaissance ~

Time Destroys Us All.

        Wisdom is wasted on the young; and Youth
is wasted on the Wise

Stations of the Cross

The bridges are bleeding this morning
and but a few have already passed on, down in a six
  foot Grave.
None are dead within Tragedy, but all . . .
  They've been sacrificed I protest! Protestations!
The final editions have been printed.

For the IV's inserted into enlightened veins flowing
unabashedly through humankind's spacetime sojourn
  picky with sunny white -- bearing of Glowing
Scribes Picketed past the Choir's seditious diatribe
Not failing his common sense but living past his
  present tense

There is no desire to see past these frames looking
  like fruitless trees
              Surrounding, depictions, artwork dreamy

            Paint the story. . . tell it chronologically, my
linear Love and Life for All desperate for the answers,
crying, for the murderers of Pilate . . .
yet no answers in-coming! Framework tells the tale.

Frame the Story. Frame the Artwork.

            His Body Hung. His Body Before a Mass,
held limp, held and bowed his head
    For all day, the sun sparkles upon the thorns, his
muscular body limp,
    the glorious head hangs down and smiles

Sunshine Beat Freestyle

The essential Sunshine enterprise provides a guide for
    good living
        and bursts a few, laughing rhymes

A statue of Homer . . . . reminds me of Blind DOOM

The Bloods of the STRONG soar through our veins,
        Rapping, stylish Freestyles:

Let it be known:

    That my eye is full of sunshine
        Who do you think is kickin' in our pictures?
Thicker, quicker, the high shit, the hot shit,
        Psychic amongst shitkickers and farm hicks
and clocks that strike the basics

                Make it true, the deaf and
the blind will hear and see again.

A Bazooka against DOOM!

    Suicide is always DOOMED . . . .

HaHaHa

    I Rise with my Brother like Phoenixes
        from the impossible odds of
impending DOOM!
Ha! I laugh in your face, Doom! Ha! Ha! Ha! Ha! Ha!

I will bathe my bare head in sunshine once
more!

and I will provide those who intercept other minds
with a way to being young again . . .

and send them reeling with their
eyes agleam:

THE DEAD WILL WALK AGAIN!

And Sunshine utter through our
splendid lips:

Don't afright of
the isolated afterlife

who
quacks and so does the infamy

Clouds floating across that Sunshine,
Saying this metaphysical statue and all
that's previously
Dead, was not really a conniving Godhead, but
rather Bred:

Because even inside of reality,
psychologically, yes....it's

ALL IN YOUR HEAD!

The Modern Desirous

They have come home now,
with their barbarous boots they
kick off the snow,
with half-awakened movements
and subconscious laughter
musing to one another
about their last days
of tentative thought.

Through the Lincoln tunnel, even in
the darkness of sleep, his headache
plagues him like a tortured philosopher.
Now, in his vision of consigned
heavenly light, cool stone tunnel,
passes through as a dimensional
portal to new worlds
unexplored.

Despite voices,
everyday as is tradition,
a small sinewy, tough, rigid,
acceptance draws on
her head, new
eternal dawns,
and gives jewelry
to the unexpected
wrist of an empress
in
America.

In a garage at 11:00 p.m. cards
are constantly being dealt,
meeting me with favorable
hands. Then on the
stoop of the front door,
an old brownstone,
whistles of the New York
night.

Your idle crisp song of garden tongues laughs
eloquently and praises
my brotherhood.
inside my
heart of
the
unknown.

Metric Song

(An Aethereus Decanto Homage to a Diggin' Evan DeCoste)

Lyrical Genesis promotes a subtle idea
>Hath not Homer's taken tales

Put your money on God!
>Let the infectious wail of Bustle sail

On these great winds we persist
>Persistence is key

Here in Denver! A blessed night unholy of unworthiness
>The Opera is getting over now

The taken women shake in the cold and talkers are
>Bustling in Societal-tongued ingestions
>Saying:

These are the last mistakes we'll ever make!

An idyllic forthright buildings planted
>In molten positions like death darts

>Brushing the translucent lumbered towers!
>Yelled great people to their Camel Taxis!

>Bring me a way home!

II. (Extra Musical Phrases)

Proclaim the many Enemies
These instants are quick
Like the days! (pause)
These are the hours of
Truth!
My dumb celebrated eyes
Take in the quirked majesty
Of stomped buildings in
Old Denver!
Whatever architect came up
With this structure
Must've not spent time in this
Dank room. My reflection is
Spilled onto the Streets
Below.

Outside the old window blows
From the new streets
Where there aren't storm grates to heat
The poor, the half-house-condo
Ignorant of proper procedures
Stoning whispers of unexpected vacancies!

O windless Genesis allow your cool raincoat worthy
Breeze blow to make the whistling

A marble breath canonized in bemusement

DREAMERS!
Don't party unless the flesh is desired~!

Les Premières Vibes Hausse d'un Nouveau Soleil

Ah, can my better glistering breath that is thou being
At last catch a glimpse of the sunset dazzl'd & reeling?
            I saith: 'my blood is rich'
            Like a tearful of ecstasy
                Painted on memory's selfish easel
                Capturing your dawn's tawny bosom

& its requisite vernal bantams

      & I think & am & therefore CAN walk the plank of
a high & mighty tank
              & have half the powerful world
in front of my hazy eyes
              & show blindness sight & turn
darkness into light
& yet then perhaps see a multitude of soulful beauties
            Fed with one loaf of bread:

A pusher of tyrannical values: O Sun! O Vibes! O Souls!

      How I am unwashed in Destiny's throes!

           Mustered, unflustered by the unwashed
cloud's deafening thunder
           & Boom & still ease the whispers &
contain'd wonders
         Of a blossoming child in thy sun-splashed & bashful
womb

As all nature's beauty is apprehended in fleshed
apparitions seated before Heaven's angelic Prince &
Hell's thin pauper . . .

--With a fist to grasp the eternity near here & there
            Amongst the Holy Dead via the day's half-
living hours . . .

                        Where I see:

Sleepy old palaces, towering flowers, a hearth of
daybreak, & night doth awake:

            & yet as idle shores of vanity's vein shone upon
the proletariat:

                        I desired to chant, proclaim & preside
o'er the unplugged Sun like a criminal or an insane Saint:

Because who here among us has no sins or commissions
to amend?

            For how can life with such an extraordinary
beginning have such an ordinary end?

A Song of Gambles

His candles had been lit for days
    Color'd & Static
Christmas Lights
  On his tree and a fireplace cracking one campfire
    with intestinal courage and admirability

Carefully, he picks up the stiletto

Ah! He sighs, without sunshine anywhere nearby.

He electrifies his hand with jabs.
    scarcely missing his ashen fingers and fingernails
He scraped his wedding ring

It being both scratched & rusted with the serrated
    doll knife.

Comfort to gambling, he gambles on . . .

        Takes a minute to inhale again from his
    filterless Camel
Smoke therefore engulfed,

A billow of smoke.

There lie his communion ready hands.
        Another Brotherly gamble
  Thinking of art and high society . . . and the
missing wedding ring finger on his other hand.

A Crying Virgil

Sharpened apt. stretch'd mirror is cracked
I haven't lived an affair in years
My image is a lice referred
Laughing an awful lot about rural jewels
Taking Troy is an endeavor of fire
My bearings need regrouping & oiling
Flying on brooms to sweep empty clouds
& all things gather dust
Music's nomenclature purifies ancient tools
Steeped in libraries full of glyphs
Harmonics gasp in dumb eras of Italy
The Pope breathes an unstained grave
Gathering the homeless playing harps
A fancy fantasy dumb utopian Raphael
Hath you sleep in your birthday cake?
Our guide is woe & envisioned
He demonstrates a faculty for high art
And illustrates God's reflection in his image

Noam Chomsky Word Salad

The foundational apparatus of institutionalized control
was certainly in the broader schematic of

say the underlying structure or model of U.G.
or generative grammar. In the broader hypothesis of say,
the sundering of minority-autonomy, there is overwhelming
historical precedent in say, the 100 years war if we
examine the statistical data analysis the fundamental
elements, properties, or aspects of U.G. or generative
grammar we find the post-zionist literature through the
lens of critical discourse studies and Descartes unfinished
work on the mathematical model of the human mind
through dispensational analyses. Now, man had no
intuitive, internal understanding of say the gravitational
constant, however, he did understand the rational,
computational basis for the C-1 interface with say, the
science of the psychology of linguistic-detailed study.
Further, the sensory-stimuli system is a finite system
and should be addressed accordingly. The organizational
language hierarchy was indexed by the cumulative
hierarchical model in set theory per Von Neumann
certainly in the 19th century. The transformational
grammar was adequate for supplying the syntactic
structures of U.G. and proved to be of infinite use for the
minimalist programs. According to something like X-Bar
theory, where A.M. Turing believed A.I. to replace the
clocks of Galileo the syntax-semantic interface is deemed
germane certainly by the rationalist standards of post-
Leninist doctrine.

However much Piaget may have shied away from
various empiricist tendencies we do find a certain amount
of latitude in the Israeli-Palestinian conflict; which is
precisely what U.S. intelligence analyzes -- now, this is a
direct attack on Obama. Congress is sending a message
to the breakdown of society through a means by which

no direct correlation can be made to any anthropological hegemony; certainly as it relates to the sundering of overall autonomy in the broader schematism of creativity or linguistic novelty. Matsou and I discussed these topicalities in an interview in Paris in the 1970s.

The New Mandarins proved inadequate in scope and time to stave off the immutable travesty of the creativity of justice versus power and the inevitable and bizarre debate with Michel Foucault. The electronic reality of the modern era is certainly owed to the consent of the consumer placed by profit over people, which is a fundamental aspect or property of U.G. or generative grammar. And as for generative poetics, I cannot discuss -- as I had nothing to do with that social mapping in the instantiation of the claim's identity-formation, conversely the infinite, and now undefined parameters of generative semantics. As a corollary, the physicist examines nature, though mathematics are an underlying aspect of linguistic deployment and performance. The post-Cartesians could not be concerned with the mathematical-physics of Pascal, certainly not in the realm of what came after. Now, 500 years of scientific inquiry has proved utterly substantial. Which is a fundamental aspect of U.G. or generative grammar, and Occupy Wall Street has been a good thing for Democracy and we'll just have to see where it goes . . .

Fedallah

Fedallah's ruptured the Colossal Claw
He hast stricked vast & ignoble Beasts!
He stands erect in a turban & flowing Purple Robes
        a sash & Parscee Ascot, --- Harpoon in Right Hand!
Looking out to infinite Seas . . .
Zoroaster exalts Ormazd!
But Ahriman is fortified in Steel
As Hearses approach by no mortal means
Reins of Black Hawks meet civil honors
Leviathan speaks its fetid noise
Asherah knows not of Yojo!
But Campagna & swamps is no match for the Sahara;
    cries God:

That which Consumeth Man, Consumeth All!

Gutter Rainbows

O but what about Love?
        I remember Love!

Love fallen down, like downfallen amber the forgotten
ashes of a misplaced loving lyre;
        lyre entwined shall be the entailing of our
disunion and unions simultaneous
Unbecoming goes pitiable sentient
The imperfection of all perfect ambitions come dead,
all too much, and all too, all of a sudden

But there!

Magnificent Atonement!

It is the City mingled with the Sun!

MoRt the Poeta, Appellation Sex Exhaust

As the poet shed his medallions
His raw annoyance seeks to release
A peach'd tongue & diffident, blue eyes
As his frenchified soulgirl moans---
Near on a trance, kisses her sores & thighs
Thru blemishes o'er a circular toil
Candles beginning to crumble & cry
& in Her slow caress he feels an
Endless ebb of a desire to sigh

Daniel; Daniel; Daniel B.

A whistle of street music enlivens the blacktopped
streets, portraying it as slightly sunburnt, as the streets
were red as naked flesh keeping out the twisted and
winding drafts, paralyzing the proletariat, and shuttering
the freezing, whose limp and nimble bodies, sifted
frost, from the playful clouds from above, winding
and whistling, a great tune, fed up with the vision as
it rises high up above the knees of the storyteller,
his mouth opened, and then closed with enormous
fission, diffusing the light of a sacred star, that fiendish
immediacy where delusion spoke of fractured beauty,
an essence of thought, a disaster of immediacy and a
denizen of languid, deteriorating intellect.

Computer Hackers, Artful

The new cowboys! The vigilantes! The beauty, O Beauty!
   Such night spread like a hemisphere,
So beautiful your binaries and deception, floating, ominous
  music
    & threats, a-Trojan ~ disembodied voices. . .
B.A. such education, immaculate. Courage. Tattoos.
Cigarettes, yank goes the hacker!
 D-DoS B.S. ~ Boom! A website fucked up. A tide turned,
like a mathematical prodigy
snorting lines of linear and non-linear algebra. D-DoS...you
ARE immense, O villains of the
    noblest Heart, - routine, immaterial...and maniacal
laughter, aloft
Shoot me in the foot and corral the rest.
 The union shall one day thank you.

Title

I want my body lying in a field so that I can be eaten.
        Let the birds eat me.
 I want my Death to come full circle with nature.
        I want to give life as I absorb Death. Yes, merci.
 R.I.P. to the posses of this world
        (and to Jim Morrison).

Book 2

AS THE SUN WEEPS

From *The Ballad of Lady Vigilance*

Frozen Sun

Sometimes I wonder how many Suns there have Been, soft, mellow tobacco balls of fire illuming the world bright with sunshine & light, & beautiful twilights, flashing their passionate gaze upon the unsuspecting world. I lay sometimes, in a hammock just to let the Sunlight sink in, I love sunlight & it provides me with a warm heart, but the Sun is frozen in time, unable to dissociate or escape, sort of like a tasteless tongue, stuck in the mouth of animal with fangs; everything equals perfect. But if that Sun doesn't last long neither will the multitudes of others surrounding it & sometimes I wish to lay down on silk or satin, jasper -- velvet even, & absorb its amorously drifting waves of permanence worthy of Latin . . . yeah.

Clouds Busting & Rains to Follow

i have drunk to your memory
But, now clouds are going to bust
Rain appears as though it has to come down
i know now to what has to be said
what do you think about me?
what now do you have to say?
i thank you for your all your Blessings
my Reality, a literal Chariot has Broken Free
. . . i bid adieu to you, as well.

Portrait of the Galaxy's Planets as They Align

So see! Sallow stars are the Sun's best friends!
        I praise & worship the Sun as a God, a clean God . . .
                Just, fair, accommodative, flaming, etc.

Hermes & the pale fumes of Venus rise like a spacious
    tsunami
        o'er indispensable dirty atmospheres (dirty w/
    pollution)

I exhale the cigarette of reality . . .

& I lose myself in the prettiness of the lunate moons of Jupiter
glistering in toiled, spatial emblems harboring no infused
tobaccos!

        Dizzy inscriptions on wind-powered EPIGRAMS!

(. . .)

The street lamps of eternity shone like the a non-pernicious
virus on the elegant planets
        as they align in a polaroid Heaven

& Earth frowns as the rest of the planets SMILE ~

A gasping, fattish moth flies into the lampshade of the Milky
    Way's mouth

& her downfallen organ-flower, lofts the timbre
eyes
phantasmal musicality . . . .
I kiss Neptune's weeping, mournful tomb mah! I am
unwilling to frown . . .
& the psalm says: Do not weigh the Sun's grandeur or
pull past the carcass of a solar floweret's darkness! ~

(A majestic bulb enjoys floating without any
gravity in the garden of orthodoxy)

The stars dance like crazy = & make hearths of gorgeous,
gaseous coins
 Out of planetary observations & configurative visions!
I would make elegiac cloaks & cassocks out of the
Martian's faint silk
& unnatural bones out of the unborn who are still
unbaptized
In a galactic-vacuum-attic's presence . . .
If I were as dreamy as you, aligning in a cosmic psychosis
I should need no pity awakenings
In your illogical, noiseless solidarity
'twould make Holy a lofty glimpse of whimsical faith
A lasting vision! Ah, but the last remaining marbles
are like stylish erudites transfixed in a mild sky!
I took my pictures . . . a photograph, lithograph, painting . . .

Then in hieroglyphical translation I swing the palatial
superfaar planet, Pluto on a carousel wing & float thru the
steamy vat & insane vacuum to join a non-diluted throne
to sit upside down amongst the stars . . .

Once the debris-tides of galaxy reach a crescendo
& all the planets marry each other & consummate their
acidic relationships & reign like that which we call
God o'er Mother Earth!

Natalya

A Bite of Vampiric, ain't ya Romanian?
That neck is for ample teeth, wrought with snowy
    flakes akin to albino skin
the more brought on by the poor Nosferatu charms
    sniffs the garlic alarm
Nobody goin it alone, your face my backwards
optimism, I am the accent perfect
You do it better
Lavander, Purple eyes crying vivid rhines, eyes bleed
    like they do on dank weed
Go to sleep, Natalya, in the morning, the A.M. you'll
    be dope
I await your teeth

Requiem For the Train Tracks

The steel trains ran so fast
 Its central theme was yesteryear
& because its galaxy exploded
  I cannot ever find ye
& a ruinous town keeps on
its careless Pastors harbor
Patriarchal fetishes like
 Clumsy Angels! Meh!
            I've seen enough of these tall graveyards!
Haunted by those Salem witches
within grey, germy skies--
Gravel spews on tarnished tracks
& Lines the toxic countryside
 & we stand chucking rocks
out onto the tracks as far
            as we can see . . .
There is a lot to gather
Eyes bloodshot, running on zero sleep
& dialects of drowsy trinity
 Tight roped to the tracks peon post
Taller & far away is an unforeseeable station
  That ported many great trains
in the years gone by---
Its wheels no longer run on flailed rails
 & oxidized eyes o'erreach
Melting in metal made of abundant
skeletal infamy--

A thousand years in the making of a new railroad

As a new dream for summer is lashed & built

   eons upon plaques

Our brattle hip's lament for

Trial witches--young Grey girls

Stirring to duly steer

 That ferocious train

closing its open mouth like a Baltic of Hell

 No axe or horse could tame

Fearing steeped old truths

Reveling in its endless miasma

All would be worth painting

On blankly skinned canvases

  Seems like all & all

That ghost-train spirit never

 dies around those worthy of its

drunken cowboy tumbleweeds

        The restive railway is blocked

Never seeking to deflect its shimmering gridiron because

There was a dark epoch--it knew

When that mystic iron hadn't been of

Virgins, Memories, Treasures

---or ever even was . . .

For Peter Tosh

A drink of Irish Moss am I
& Pot soaked capillaries
A resurrection of Jesus in Ethiopia

O how you'd love to legalize Love & God

Tobacco and your lady friends back back in Kingston
  Fuse the sunlight on the blackest hair
                    Twirling those dreadlocks, that hair,
                    that hair

Stumbling, I stop to glare, at an impasse
                With your alcoholic sweats
and make some new fortifying whiskey
                & bring home the treble, clef, and bass

            Smoking kush into lungs of tar

Until the fallen angels sing of illuminations

                    ....and we wade in the waters
of the Caribbean . . .

Reconstructions

1.

The Stars are all webbed together tangled in the cobwebs
of an orchestrated estate that speaks in rustic truths in an
extinct dialect of immaculacy, and yet I have survived!
But I do not wish to brag.

2.

She was still infantile when child was born, at sixteen
no less. The facsimile of care.

3.

Bathing dust, asoak like shackles everlasting

4.

I lick the exposures to the ancient lyre's musky scents

5.

The sky was as blue as a Heaven I could imagine . . .

6.

They have touched my fancy, in a million strings of
vaudeville. The billiard room, like Newton, hoists numeric
green cloth o'er deft hands and tepid water.

7.

A Howl dying not far from its trenchant desire.

8.

Tears of confusion cleanse rough fingers, small
delicate fingers . . . O, would you look at those fingers!

Those skeletal hands, blessed with the fingers of a pianist!

9.

When you're at a Grand Piano, you're obligated to sit
down and fuck around.

Harmonicas

When the wind goes sailing
I skip down lucky lanes
  . . . back ag'en in Venice in powdery drawl
I pass patrons in Pubs, drinking their Pints
 thru my own Eyes
Everyday people breaking note filled harmonicas for a Euro
......dropped in a glass of emotional affluence.

A Crucifix Life

Stacked I'll be in the Church Square
Attached to a Hanging Cross
Floating down a bubbly, bubbly water alley in Venice
I feel as though I am but a Child, sleeping

...and said great men stranded on bridgelessness above
who creep home to the hour of windy music
Rowing, rowing, rowing, rowing, I go I go go go go Go.

The opponents plop out the window at Midnight
to scatter their tan tinged feet along for silhouetted sky
    above
and when I look back at these conscienceless followers

I scratch the sleepless eyes thereof.

Electric Eyes

Staring, Glaring, Bloodshot, Bleeding.
  Neither alive, neither Dead.
a telepathic deconstruction . . .
            Angry, dysphoric, manic
euphoric, hateful invectives fill the airs circl'd round
      and round
  staring, and stumbling and stop to glare
stoned, catatonic stupor, parkinsonian-like,
jagged eyes, eyes that penetrate, like a slut seducing
Logic, magnetism, illogical conceits, bold
Bolder eyes, still, craving, mad mad eyes
Eyes like Roman Candles, and capillaries red like
      Vietnamese Spiders
angry and crawling, slithering their way into the other
      Brain
Piercing, Piercing, Piercing thru and thru, to and to
  from to from,
front to back back to front side to front side back and
      back to side and front to front
            Alas! Your final affront to my conscience! I'm
done being harrassed.
A Slap in the Face.

Endless Points

Graph. Theorem.

Here it goes:

Let O -= o < O (H), so point, in problems yet to be
solved. yet how many points?

I count a perfect celestial sphere, the perfect Geometric
      Poetry
            Euclidean, beautiful, numerical, and analytical
Modern, Ancient, Anthropological, Cultural Meccas of
      Number Lines.

2.

Inversion, the points infinite, the point finite . . . grease
pencils adorn
            amid bipolar mania, O > little o H has many
conceivable points,
and the graph in between, the symbols, O pictograph
and pictures, I chant planes!
But do not fly and zounds adhere, x = y y=s

Greater than. Pictograph

Insert Images Here. ala Cantos

The Vampyre's Knife

A strife knife of angled teeth
folds its chin and extends - -
drifts twelve saliva splashes
On the pale-abdicate flesh
and slowly bends down
Girl still asleep and to touch
penetrates her neck
        Thinking of her old boyfriend...

Accent

I cried a yellow, sunless tear in the mist of a rain of
    exhaust
& I captured the sighs of the Sphinx & the estranged
    w/ a joyful gaze
Grasping a useful dialect dubbed repentance &
    forgetful nostalgia
I seal'd my treasures in an ethnic vase . . .
After I arrived on the illogical steps of immortality in
    extravagance
The steps of the disquiet'g riot, a mad, fairy knell,
    destiny ~
I then knew that there was no marriage between life
    & the afterlife
Hanged back before the undead, frozen, ill
How sad, how maladroit the sad despotism of
    frightful dawns
for what justice is there when the sun of promise &
    the luxury
in between is ablaze w/ villains, vandals, & vagrants!
A holy infallible trinity, disengaged becomes a
    lethally mark'd knuckle sandwich
in its steel constraints of frightful pawns
How dead is the infamy when the ground is foreign,
    cold, bereft of spirits
& the justice upon transgression is augment'd, aye---
The sybaritic winds knew not to blow the seed of the
    desert
Where none before stood, where no psalm is known
    to sunsets

For even w/ my skeletal frame ascrib'd w/ black &
    bluish nausea
I arrive on a physical & immobile sand dune
God permits the law & I defy it
O past lore! O Golden Sun! O delirious, babbling Sun!
But those who wear cassocks know no vacancies of heart
I heard incessant screams of celestial & beautiful pariahs
    like knights
She dances there, in a garden, in her heart still full of
    tranquil anonymity
As the smoke rises from the snot of the Red Sea
I see the lost angels o'er the hillside near the tweak'd
    crystal meth sky
Immovable glaciers of invisible promise awaken the filthy,
    unkempt dead
I trek & thresh like war lest Father Winter fracture &
    absorb his hellish sands!
& faithful I opt to pluck each eyelash like a skanky dynamo
Above, God fractures the red skies w/ orange thunderbolts
I pray'd for she who left hell & beheld the world anew in
    the vegetation of an Afric eve
Flaming intently w/ the nest of virtuous souls & the lost
Gods hath been bereft of violence quelled by pride---
Screaming sacred hieroglyphic verses like dolorous
    hailstones!
A flying palla sea eagle interrupts its somber rhyme
& I hang back before this girl, unsure yet unafraid
But I bless'd her heavenly affections there on the dusk of
    a new world in atonement
& she was flashed upon the red leaf & the darkling sky
& soon behind thee, half-awaken'd lay the unbroken dye,
    as a ghostly rebel squawked

Hoping to amass the unlit ruin of listless faith
& I in sunken majestic sofa, half-dead, drunk &
awaiting execution desire:
A haze of green, an eye in the ocean of frozen bath
deserts
Where into the perfumed twilight I full of starkly
abbreviated astonishment procure:
A jade as fragile as a star twinkling in the Milky Way

A Fragmented Memory from the Mind of Dionysus!

...a great orgy last night he was drunk now hung over
taxis of the Ancients pass by his window
he breathes heavily as cockroaches sow seeds of viral
    infections
a note, a musical phrase a slight inflection of notable
    salience
drifts from the frosty breath of his tar tinged lungs
parched with dry indifference, a sandy cusp of loose
    dusky visions, inaugural
shit . . . he says, no more blood to drink from lost whores
i must be a venereal disease or possess one, here
to drop me off at the Atbarah ye say
drunk, staggering, etc. O let the Sails of the Warm Weather
    take ye away on the Nile
i am so sick of Cities! i am so sick of Culture, he thinks,
    brooding a nefarious sentimentality
the cold rain of exhaust has brought my symbols to both
    power & defeat
metropolitan city gutters will bring back poor memories
he realizes O, the requirement of a seaside breeze
no more of this albatross can ye exist, no more!
he lights up a cigarette, coolly.
& in penultimate vanity he watched as the small houses
    of the Vista
Upset, Uproot, & tumble thru the Air,
like Small Children o'er the Crystalline Sunset,
forever banished from THIS Eternity.

Like by the Severn River; Nostalgia Laid Bare

It has been spoken that there is nothing more healing than human affection.
Life, splayed open, is like an incessant river of time; and if we're not careful, we might drown

Yes, Smiles Expiate Like Good Medicine!

Smiling can make you happy
All it takes to smile is to smile
The act of smiling can bring great joy
Smiling more helps everyone
If you are sad, I recommend smiling

Alexej Savreux was born in Burlington, Vermont, and grew up in the northeastern and southwestern U.S. Savreux is a longtime resident of both Kansas City, KS and Kansas City, MO. Savreux is a poet, satirist, and critic with an academic background in linguistics, communications/journalism, film, physics, theater tech, and information technology. He owns and operates illogical conceits multimedia, a DIY media, and technological communications sole prop out of his apartment in Kansas City, MO. Savreux has served on the advisory board of Kansas City PBS, the artistic committees of NoDivideKC, and the Kansas City Electronic Music and Arts Alliance (KcEMA). His publications have appeared in periodicals as diverse as *Psychology Today*, *KC Studio*, *ScholarSpace*, and *The Pitch*. He is a 2016 Writer's Digest winner, a 2021 Shakespeare Prize Winner, and a 2022 recipient of an NEA Special Project Grant for the Centerpieces For Social Justice exhibit at InterUrban Arthouse. He divides his time between Kansas City and New York.

This project was made possible, in part, by generous support from the Osage Arts Community.

Osage Arts Community provides temporary time, space and support for the creation of new artistic works in a retreat format, serving creative people of all kinds — visual artists, composers, poets, fiction and nonfiction writers. Located on a 152-acre farm in an isolated rural mountainside setting in Central Missouri and bordered by ¾ of a mile of the Gasconade River, OAC provides residencies to those working alone, as well as welcoming collaborative teams, offering living space and workspace in a country environment to emerging and mid-career artists. For more information, visit us at www.osageac.org

Osage Arts Community